AUTUMN
gnomes

coloring book

AUTUMN
gnomes

AUTUMN
gnomes

AUTUMN
gnomes

AUTUMN gnomes

AUTUMN gnomes

AUTUMN gnomes

AUTUMN
gnomes

AUTUMN
gnomes

hello
FALL

AUTUMN
gnomes

hello
FALL

AUTUMN
gnomes

Fall

AUTUMN
gnomes

AUTUMN
gnomes

AUTUMN
gnomes

AUTUMN
gnomes

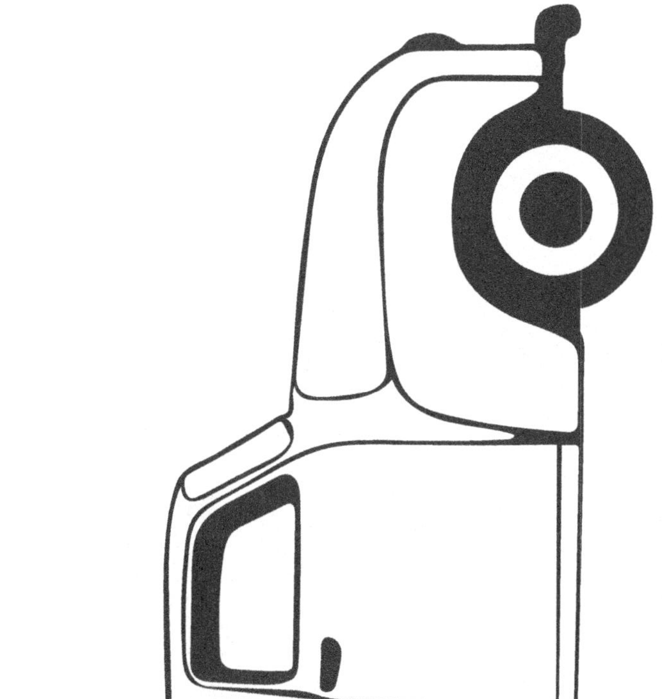

AUTUMN gnomes

AUTUMN gnomes

AUTUMN
gnomes

AUTUMN
gnomes

AUTUMN
gnomes

AUTUMN

AUTUMN
gnomes

AUTUMN
gnomes

AUTUMN
gnomes

AUTUMN
gnomes

AUTUMN
gnomes

AUTUMN
gnomes

Hello
autumn

AUTUMN gnomes

AUTUMN
gnomes

AUTUMN
gnomes

Fall

AUTUMN
gnomes

AUTUMN
gnomes

AUTUMN
gnomes

Made in the USA
Las Vegas, NV
30 September 2023

78352227R00037